SERIOUS BUSINESS

INSIGHTS FROM A 5-YEAR-OLD

BY TINA SMOTHERS

Published in Des Moines, Iowa, by:
Bookpress Publishing
P.O. Box 71532
Des Moines, IA 50325
www.BookpressPublishing.com

BookPress®
www.BookpressPublishing.com

Publisher's Cataloging-in-Publication data
Names: Smothers, Tina, author.
Title: Serious Business : Insights from a 5-year-old / by Tina Smothers.
Description: Des Moines, IA: BookPress Publishing, 2024.
Identifiers: ISBN: 978-1-960259-07-3
Subjects: LCSH Success in business—Humor. | Management—Humor. | Humor. | BISAC HUMOR / Topic / Business & Professional
Classification: LCC HF5386 .S66 2024 | DDC 650/.1—dc23

First Edition
Printed in the United States of America
10 9 8 7 6 5 4 3 2 1

iNTRODUCTiON:

In life and business, five-year-old Maverick lives up to his name. He has listened in on thousands of hours of business calls, has taken notes on countless business meetings, and has spent a lifetime observing his mother, Tina Smothers, speaking up with the no-holds-barred attitude required for entrepreneurial success. Now an expert on the tricks of the trade, Mav is ready to enlighten the business world with his most cutting-edge wisdom on how to properly run a business.

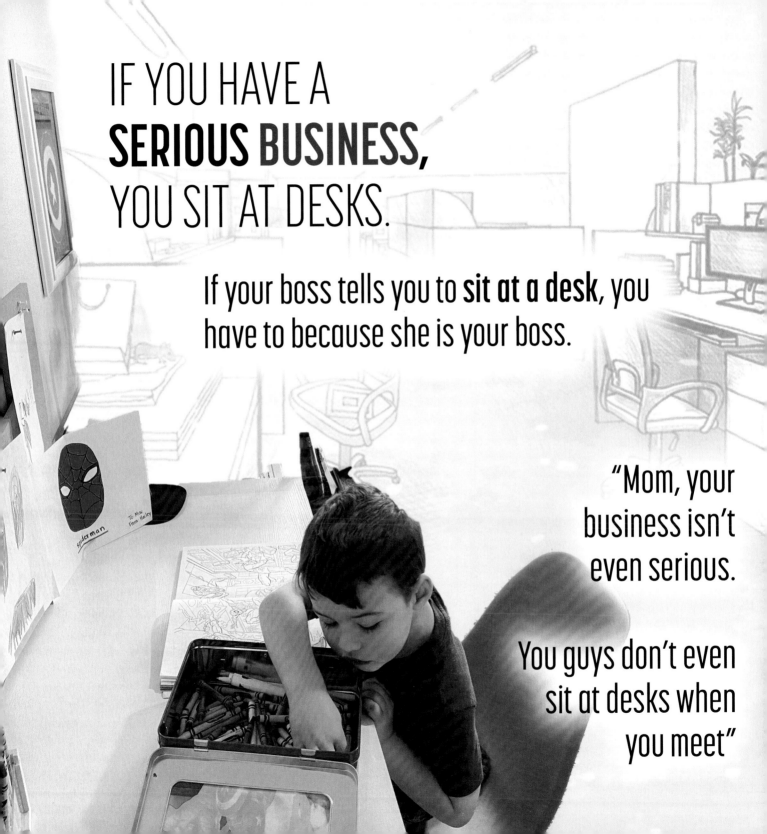

IF YOU HAVE A **SERIOUS** BUSINESS, YOU SIT AT DESKS.

If your boss tells you to **sit at a desk**, you have to because she is your boss.

"Mom, your business isn't even serious.

You guys don't even sit at desks when you meet"

IN A
SERIOUS BUSINESS,
YOU NEED A
GOOD HEADSHOT.

A headshot is shoulders-up, so you can wear whatever you want on the bottom.

Also, **YOU NEED A GOOD SMILE**.

IF YOU WANT TO BE **SERIOUS** ABOUT YOUR **BUSINESS**, DON'T PACK PRETZEL GOLDFISH FOR LUNCH OR A SNACK.

You spend **TOO MUCH TIME CHEWING AND DRINKING** because your mouth is dry.

Then you can't talk business or it takes too long to eat with all the dryness and you can't get back to **SERIOUS BUSINESS.**

Just pack a fruit. It's an easy chew-and-swallow.

SOMETIMES IN A **SERIOUS** BUSINESS, YOU SET A PRETEND MEETING WITH SOMEONE.

Pick the name of someone you like a lot. That is who your meeting is with.

Then **ALL YOUR IDEAS** are awesome.

IN A **SERIOUS** BUSINESS, YOU HAVE TO PICK THE PEOPLE THAT WILL SIT WITH YOU

because you only have **SO MANY CHAIRS.**

SOMETIMES IN A **SERIOUS** BUSINESS, YOU NEED A MAGNIFYING GLASS

so you can really **STUDY WHAT PEOPLE ARE DOING.**

My mom's on a call, so **I'M IN CHARGE.**

IF YOU HAVE A **SERIOUS BUSINESS**, YOU ALWAYS HAVE SOMEONE ELSE BE IN CHARGE WHEN YOU'RE GONE.

IF YOU HAVE A **SERIOUS BUSINESS,** YOU PUT YOUR NAME ON STUFF PEOPLE WILL USE,

NOT CRAP THAT THEY JUST **TAKE AND THROW AWAY.**

(YAY, SOCK PUPPETS!)

IF YOU HAVE A **SERIOUS** BUSINESS, YOU WILL WANT TO SEE IF YOU CAN ADD SERVICES

so you can **MAKE MORE MONEY.**

WHEN YOU'RE A KID, IT'S OKAY TO CRY WHEN YOU LOSE, BUT WHEN YOU HAVE A **SERIOUS BUSINESS**,

YOU CAN'T LOSE.
You just keep working.

WHEN YOU HAVE A **SERIOUS** BUSINESS, YOU ARE IN CHARGE.

If you don't **TELL PEOPLE HOW TO ACT**, then it's your own fault.

IN A **SERIOUS** BUSINESS, YOU NEED TO GET PAID WHEN YOU DO STUFF FOR PEOPLE.

Otherwise, **YOU'RE WORKING FOR FREE,**

and you can't run a business that way.

IN A **SERIOUS** BUSINESS, YOU HAVE TO SOMETIMES SLOW THINGS DOWN IF YOU WANT THINGS RIGHT.

I just don't have time to slow down because **I have to get things done.**

So seriously, do you want it right now or done right?

"Mav, do you want to swim after lunch?"

"What? No! I'm working today, and I came up to take a short break.

That means you see what's up but **KEEP YOUR MIND ON WORK TO GET STUFF DONE.**"

If the **"CHA CHA SLIDE"** is playing next,

YOU HAVE TO CHOOSE BETWEEN DANCING AND RUNNING A **SERIOUS** BUSINESS.

WHEN YOU GO TO AN OPEN HOUSE, TAKE A SACK OF CANDY

so you can sell it to everyone in the room to **MAKE MONEY**.

LEARN TO RIDE A BIKE ON A BEAT-UP BIKE.

Then work your business a little more because you want a bright and shiny new bike to **SHOW YOUR NEW SKILLS**.

ABOUT THE AUTHOR

Tina Smothers's inspiring life journey is one of resilience, dedication, and commitment to her family, her professional aspirations, and her community. Being a mother of three and amassing an impressive twenty-seven years of experience in property management and real estate, Tina exemplifies commitment and determination. She decided to start her own business when she was pregnant with Maverick.

Maverick learned about business intricacies by accompanying Tina on her daily commute and while enduring the 'work from home' model in 2020. The value of learning from experience and exposure is evident in Maverick's business sensibilities.

Tina is appreciative of her husband Rich, daughter Xyola and son's McCoy and Maverick for their patience of her "Lula 15" as she always pushes to get just one more thing done for the business.

Beyond business, Tina passionately advocates for suicide and mental health awareness and she supports locally owned businesses contributing to the empowerment and growth of her community.

ABOUT THE SERIOUS BUSINESS PARTNER FOUNDER

Maverick is now enjoying enjoying his 7th year of life at home in Iowa with his brother and parents. He enjoys FaceTiming with his sister in Chicago. Remaining highly competitive at anything he does is a constant for Mav. Completing 18+ Lego sets are a top priority. He continues to shine daily, speaking as he speaks exactly what he thinks in a confident, loud voice. Mav is on a mission to enlighten others to be Serious in a positive way personally and professionally.